ISBN-13: 978-1480228078

For information address:

info@lessalmon.com

www.lessalmon.com

THE AUTHOR
Les salmon

A proud father of two daughters Les is an ex soldier, soccer player, stunt man, engineer, artist… the list goes on.

He has travelled the world teaching a myriad of sports and activities.

Skiing has dominated his winters taking him from working in Scotland through; Austria, Italy, France, Sweden and Colorado.

His summers have seen him; lead treks across Africa, teach; sailing, windsurfing and scuba diving in the St Tropez area, Horse riding in the French Alps, Tennis in Sweden and France (He ran his own tennis school in France) guided and ran his own Hill Walking tours of the Scottish Highlands. In recent times he has gone back to the passion of his youth and he coaches soccer.

His background in teaching activities and sport led him to write his book Myths, Lies and Skiing. The book has been lauded by the Austrians and described as "The most inspirational ski book" and "A priceless jewel."

Since 2007 he has been running ski tours to The Alps and Colorado.

For Natalie & JoAnne

CONTENTS

THE BEGINNING

For me working as a ski teacher started out as a cheap way to ski and earn a bit of cash while at college. The idea of doing it as a career never entered my head. So what happened? Read on...

I had just spent the summer working in the St Tropez area of the French Riviera. I arrived back at college with great memories, a tan and...broke.

The previous winter I had gone skiing a few Sundays at Glenshee. This is a ski area about an hour from my home town of Perth (the 'original' to any Aussies out there) Saying I had gone skiing is a bit of a glamorous moniker as most of the time was spent

1. Trekking from the car park to the slope and back again. This alone took up about half the day.

2. Climbing up the slope for 10 minutes for a 10 second slide down! (as one wag commented it sounded like my sex life!) When you add the getting up bit after the falling down bit, I figure that in the whole day I probably spent about a quarter of an hour on the actual sliding down the hill bit.

Finally, completely knackered, we had the joy of walking all the way back to the car park and bus.

Not a few times this was all done in the rain! (There is a reason Scotland and Ireland are green!)

For those of you who haven't enjoyed our lovely weather, Scotland has rain, snow and every combination of them both. It then throws in a wee quirk...it all tends to arrive 'horizontally!'

Years ago they installed a snow cannon. Proud as punch they stood around for the great switch on. Pride before the fall as they could only watch on in consternation as their manufactured snow was pumped into the pristine Scottish air only to be high-jacked some 20 feet up where the wind wheeched it off on a 90 degrees 'exit stage right' direction towards the Russian Steppes. Never to be seen again.

WHOOOSH!!

The Scots donating snow to Russia.

Actually the very first time I had attempted skiing was about five years previously. I went with the local Perth ski club. They used to run a bus to Glenshee on Sundays.

The bus trip up was an adventure on its own. At that time there was a bend in the road called 'The Devils elbow' and we'd have to get out of the bus and push! The journey back was good too as negotiating the afore mentioned bend going down was a great constipation cure.

Half way home we'd stop and at a watering-hole for a tea dance. The usual venue for us was at a hotel in the village of Blairgowrie. There we'd be at the bar with our damp clothes streaming away nicely. It was a sock dance so we left our ski boots in the hall…god only knows what it smelled like but it was cosy. Once we had stunk the place up enough…we'd leave. A great end to the day.

I was now hooked on skiing. I loved it. The question that was bugging me now was, how can I afford to do it again this winter?

I never dreamt that I was going to become part of the scene.

I was in the bar with some friends trying to figure out what kind of job I could do to earn some extra cash to go skiing. The last term I had worked in a local Hotel doing quick portraits of their guests. It was okay but that was mainly weekend work and that would kinda interfere with any plans to ski.

Out of the blue one of the guys in a matter of fact way says

'Why not go up and work part time as an instructor?' As if it was a perfectly obvious solution.

'Yeah right. I've skied about nine days in my life so I'm obviously over qualified for the job.' I said somewhat sarcastically.

"No listen, you'd only be working Saturdays and Sundays" He pressed on. "How much damage could you do in two days?"

The more beers we had and the more we talked about it the more the idea appealed. Because of my military experience I was used to teaching and being in control of groups of people. If I only got people that had *never* skied before it was doable. Now could I get one of the ski schools to bite?

A couple of weeks later I set off, up to Aviemore, the main ski area cum resort in Scotland. I had never been there before and just wandered around the centre until I saw a sign for the Cairdsport Ski School. Fingers crossed, bum clenched, I knocked on the office door.

I met the boss, Derek Brightman. A great guy, a real gentleman and one of Scottish Skiing's legends. (This guy skied down the Eiger!!) I put my weekend idea to him and to my total surprise he said okay. That was it and just like that my life was taking off in a new direction...again.

At this point, although it wasn't a conscious decision, the dye was cast...

There are two ways to do things you like.

One is to get a good job and earn and save enough to do the things you like in your spare time. The other is to work at your hobbies.

The second way usually means that you'll never amass a lot of money but you'll have a whole lot of fun along the way.

Guess which I chose?

Clues...I'm broke, but I smile and laugh a lot.

THE FIRST WEEKEND

My College money had come through and so like any self respecting student I immediately went out and bought some books….Yeah right…of course not, I bought myself an old banger of a car. It was a one of the original old boxy Vauxhall Vivas. (It was to become a story in itself.) This was to be my trusty steed for the coming season my chariot that would take me to and from Aviemore.

As it happens I got it just in time as I got a call from the ski school in the middle of November. Could I come up the following weekend as the they had a college group up from England and the ski schools full time teachers weren't scheduled to start until December. Most of them were still tied up with summer commitments. A big gulp and then I answered "Okay."

I duly arrived in Aviemore the following Friday night and met the other instructor Paul (Pavel) It was a small group and Paul was to take the people who had skied a bit and I would deal with the 'never-evers.'

The first day in skiing involves very little actual skiing. Also at the start of the season in Scotland a fair whack of the lesson is used in a fair trek across the heather to find a patch of snow. This patch of snow would be staked out at lunch time in case some 'oink' tries to muscle in! Then it's all putting on skis, taking them off, how to get up, climbing up, getting up from a fall...etc

Fortunately the group that Paul had wasn't much better than the lot I had so while I was doing my thing I was also watching Paul and learning what, effectively, would be my 'tomorrows lesson. Thankfully it turned out fine. The crowd were great bunch and we had a hoot. They had actually learned a bit and everyone (me too) had survived. I was hooked,

At he end of the second day (when the group had gone) bravado almost cost me my hundred percent survivor record. The near casualty...me!

"Lets ski down." Said Paul and like the idiot I am I heard myself say. "OK."

Now Paul was a skier and me... I was a turnip. But I was game. Off we went.

Most of the way down was on untracked snow and thankfully Paul couldn't or at least didn't look behind at me as I careened down the mountain. It must have looked like something out of the Keystone Cops. I hung in but I have no idea how. We finally got to the well packed path that led from just above the middle station (The Sheiling) to the car park. With relief I relaxed a bit and I copied Paul as he got into the downhill racer's tuck. I was safe...wrong!!!

We were approaching the Sheiling and were cooking

along nicely. I watched Paul, some fifty meters in front of me, disappear around the building. Starting to relax and enjoy myself I whizzed towards the building.

With visions of Robert Redford in the movie 'Downhill Racer' running in my head I zoomed round the Sheiling and got the scare of my life as I was hurtling straight for a bleedin' reindeer! There it was, stood bang in the middle of the track. It didn't even move as I whistled past, missing it by inches, it just raised it's head gave me a very unimpressed disdainful look. While I performed all sorts of contortions trying to miss the beast and stay upright, it resumed it's munching!

Eventually I regained a modicum of composure and I made it to the car park. Miraculously still in one piece. So trying to look as nonchalant as I could I finished my first stint as a ski instructor.

The weekend had been a success. I'd had a hoot. Derek had been satisfied and said he looked forward to seeing me again when the season started proper in December. Before he could change his mind I had picked up my money and was headed back down the A9 to Perth. This (sans the deer) was to be my modus operandi for the rest of the winter.

TEACHING SKIING
ON THE CAIRNGORMS

Aviemore has it's own unique challenges for ski teachers and they start with the first snowfall.

Aviemore is somewhat unique as the actual ski slopes are situated on the Cairngorm Mountain some seven miles away. This distance and the Scottish weather can create their own wee problems. Even when we got good snowfalls we'd be frequently stymied by the wind. This would keep us on the lower slopes or force us to use other alternatives. Aye we're adaptable as well as hardy.

THE PATCH.

This usually came about when we could actually make it to the car park by the bottom lift. Collecting your group you'd scan out an appropriate patch. Seeing one that would accommodate your group you'd charge off and I do mean charge. There were dozens of classes all looking for a 'Patch' The quicker you got organized the closer your patch was going to be. It must have been a hoot to watch. All these instructors shepherding their groups across the peat bogs to get a 'Patch.' Once found it was jealously guarded. Sentries were posted when you went to lunch... I jest not.

The ski instructor's manual says that beginners should have a run-out. That is to say that they should have terrain that will bring them to a stop naturally...good plan...only a theorist could come up with that one. We had our own natural stops...peat bogs. Skis don't slide well once they're off the snow. It does mean skiers tend to get a bit muddy.

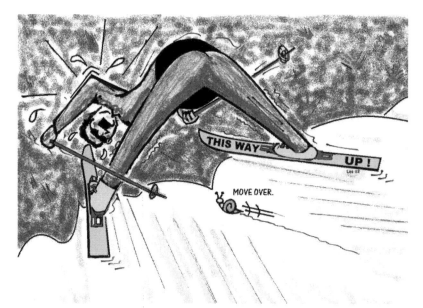

LOOKING FOR A PLACE TO FALL!

THE WIND

From the 'Patch' upwards the wind comes into play. We Brit's do go out in some filthy weather. I coach soccer in Colorado and you'd be surprised how often parents will phone up to see if training is still on as it is raining?

The first time I got such a phone call I thought it was a send up. I've had a hoot watching their faces as I'd tell them about spending hours clearing snow away from a football penalty area so we could have a kick around, or that our Mums used to have to come and drag us out of the rain, and we'd be kicking and screaming about it!! I must have sounded like a bad 'Monty Python' skit. The fact is that in Scotland if we waited for good weather we'd end up doing nothing. So a wee breeze isn't going to deter us...is it?

HEY MISTER IS THIS WHERE WE GET LESSONS?

It certainly didn't stop us going onto the slopes. 40knot wind, gusting to 60+knots...nae bother. We'd be out there. We may be leaning over at an angle of forty five degrees, but we'd be there.

As an instructor you'd line your group up with their backs to the wind. You'd get them to bind really close together, this created a bit of a wind- break for the teacher. (Well we're not complete idiots) Hunkered over your ski-poles you'd be happily teaching away.

We humans are amazingly adaptable. It doesn't take long for us to get accustomed to the constant wind. That is when mother nature shows her Steven King sense of humour. As the teacher you see it coming. You watch the effects of a gust sneaking its way towards you. It's akin to watching the shark's fin in the movie Jaws. Like the shark it stalks its way silently toward the group. Slowly it gathers speed Then... Wham!! it strikes.

As you're facing the incoming gust you instinctively bow your head into the wind. When it passes and you raise your head you see the effects that a 60knot gust of wind has had on your group of beginners. It's amazing. One minute they're making you a wonderful wind-break then WHOOOSH! they're gone!! They are now decorating the hill in amazing places and postures.

It would take about a quarter of an hour of working like a wee Border Collie to usher them all back into their windbreak mode.

Repeat this several times a day...oh it's great fun.

The Artificial Ski Slope

Sometimes we were forced to stay in the village and use the artificial ski slope next to the Post House. From what I remember (but don't quote me) the slope was about 60 feet by 25 feet. We would have about 60 (yes 60) people all trying to learn to ski at the same time on this postage stamp of a ski mat. Two groups of 'Never-evers' would be walking at the bottom. Two Beginner snow-plough groups about half way up and two quasi intermediate groups occupied the upper part of the mat. Six groups in total. They'd get an hour then the next 60 would have their turn and it went on like this throughout the day. Amazing.

The Other

It's fair to say that in the 70s many ski resorts (worldwide) never thought about global warming. It was not in the consciousness of many people and the assumption was that snow would always be there come the winter. I believe that when Cairsport introduced the alternative to skiing they pointed the way forward for Aviemore. Back then however we couldn't envisage a day when people would head to the Alps and snow on the hills would always be assured.

The alternatives were limited but it was innovative. They were also included in the cost of the lesson. Effectively the first activity 'Multi-pass' system. So on days when the hill was closed. We could offer our groups; Ski Movies, Play Curling or Visit a Distillery. The instructor would organize it all for their group.

Movies. We showed them in the 'Chalet's' office. These Chalets were situated behind the ice rink. I got my first insight into skiing outside of Scotland from them. The choice of movies was limited. Mainly they were made by; Salomon, Dick Barrymore and Warren Millar. We watched powder skiing in the Rockies or Franz Klammer win the downhill in Innsbruck. Inspiring stuff, after watching them we couldn't wait to get back on the slopes. In our heads we'd be skiing in the Canadian Bugaboos while our bodies were careening down 'Corrie Cas!'

The Distillery. Taking the group to the distillery was a nice wee jaunt. After the instructors had done their first 'How we make the stuff' tour they would let subsequent groups do the tour and wait for them in the 'Hospitality room.'

One of the distilleries had decorated their hospitality room with all the wood panelling from a ship. It s beautiful. I liked their whisky too and as you can imagine by the time the group would reappeared the instructor would have had quite a bit of hospitality.

Curling. We would normally get a lane for the group and we'd have to have a 'buffer' lane. This was to save the real Curling enthusiast. We'd get some jaundice looks from them. Especially when an errant stone oft wended it's way in their direction!

I didn't realise that it was a dangerous game. I was doing the brushing bit. Trying to look as if I knew what was doing. Zipping down the rink brushing the ice in front of the stone for all I was worth when the young lady opposite, who was also engaged in furious brushing, slipped. Up came her brush and caught me a beauty, right under the chin...WALLOP! Down I went.

I have to be one of the few people to have
been knocked out while playing...curling!?

BEN

As you read through the following stories you'll hear of some great characters. One of the recurring joys in my life are the people that I've come into contact and become friends with.

Ben was a Londoner. He had his own haulage company down in the 'Smoke' but he left a manager in charge of the business while he came up to Aviemore to work the winter as a ski teacher.

He was usually the first face that I would see when I arrived in resort every Friday night. I'd be entering the 'Illicit Still' Bar just as Ben and his group finished dinner and had repaired to the bar.

"This is my friend Les." He would beam to his group.
"He's a poor student so get him drunk!".... and they did.
Every time they bought a round I was included. It was their last night in the resort so it was a party. A great start to the weekend!

Ben had dark curly hair and a 'Biker' moustache. He'd usually be dressed in a black velvet jacket looking for all the world like the actor Peter Wyndgarde in his Jason King role. This was a TV. spy series that was popular at the time. He looked more like management than a ski instructor. This he used this to great advantage from time to time

Every winter 'The Johnny Walker Curling Championships' was held in Aviemore. This was a major International Curling competition. For a week the resort was inundated with people walking around festooned in badges and carrying brushes.

One group of competitors innocently wandered into the Illicit bar and they were immediately they were accosted by Ben.

"I'm so glad you've arrived." he chirped. leading them to a corner of the bar and started giving them cleaning instructions for the bar.

"We've been waiting ages for you cleaners to get here" He went on.

"Can you just get that corner cleaned up and then..." He chuntered on not giving the hapless curlers a chance to interrupt.

The look on the curler's faces was priceless. They thought he was the manager. He was happily ignoring their protests that he was mistaken and that they weren't cleaners. It was a hilarious. He kept it going brilliantly 'til it finally dawned on the Curlers that he was sending them up. I have to say that they took it great stead. He had held the bar spellbound. Great fun.

He also created a bit of a stir on the hill. For the folks who don't know the area Aviemore in that era it had a two-man chairlift from the car park to the middle station (The Sheiling) It was an odd arrangement as it was a skis off and carry them on affair. Then sitting side by side and facing 'Sideways' you trundled up the mountain. It's the only one of it's ilk that I've every seen. People in the know always sat on the downhill seat using the other passenger as a windbreak.

The line for the lift was usually huge first thing in the morning and it could take over an hour to get on it. Rather than wait most of the ski teachers would walk up in ski boots, carrying their skis. We were a hardy bunch!

Also it meant we could have a tea and a bun at The Sheiling while we waited for our pupils.

One day Ben scandalised the hill. No walking for him. So piling as many instructors as he could into his Range Rover we drove up to the Shieling.

There were instructors in every nook and cranny of the car. Ben couldn't reach the gear stick. I was sitting astride the damned thing so that was my job. He'd drop the clutch, give me a shout and I'd manoeuvre the stick. (I became quite adept at this as we were to employ this modus operandi on numerous occasions, including one memorable journey to Newtonmore where Helmut was showing his 'holiday snaps'...but that's another story)

BEN'S BREAKFAST EXPRESS

The look on peoples' faces when we all piled out at the Cafe...priceless.

Needless to say the management took a dim view and signs and bans were promptly put into place. Halcyon days. Thanks Ben mate.

A classic tale of Ben happened later in the season. It was in February. I was getting more experience and was asked to come up and work during the half term school holidays. Two whole weeks.

Aviemore itself is about seven miles from the Cairngorm Mountain (the mountain that you actually ski on) and the weather on the hill can be at complete odds with that of the village. Often we would be sitting in our unofficial office The Illicit Still bar and look out to see the Cairngorm Mountain looking beautiful. All white and framed with a pristine blue sky. It looked serene and stately but with a wind gusting at 60+ knots per hour it was a wild place. So technical discussions in the bar were normally the order of the day.

One day we had a heck of a time trying to convince some clients that we couldn't ski with winds that high.

"Why not? I've been in strong wind before." One girl asserted.

No matter how much we tried to explain she was not to be convinced that 60+ knots was a wee bit more than 'a strong wind. The phrase "Not for turning." comes to mind...maybe she went on to become Lady Thatcher's speech writer.

After much to and fro-ing we decided to drive her up the hill. Off we went As we got towards the top end of the chairlift's car park the van was getting well and truly battered. She was still unconvinced so we let her out. She stood there looking triumphant...that is until a wee gust came along and WHOOSH!!!... She was gone. We got her back in the car but by then the lady had not just turned, she'd thrown in a couple o' summersaults too.

NOW DO YOU BELIEVE IT'S TOO WINDY?

I digress...back to Ben and his major gaffe.

When I said the 'Illicit' was our office I wasn't too far off. The ski school had a changing room and ski hire office in the Posthouse Hotel. The ski instructors was would meet outside here before driving up the hill. The bar was an arduous 15 metre walk from our changing room. Tough life...eh?

On this particular day there was a heavy, dark, low cloud, rainy, snowy day. The valley was well and truly 'socked in' and none of us were looking forward to trudging up the hill. Ben however was in the hotel beaming.

"What are you so smug about?" We asked.

"Well while you ones will be out in this miserable weather I will be here in the bar snug and warm enjoying myself. I've told my group that the weather and visibility on the hill will be atrocious. Well if it's like this here it'll be really horrible up there," he explained.

"So we'll be staying here keeping the bar staff company." He added with a big grin. He waved us off as we grumbled our way into the van and set off to the slopes.

Poor Ben was about to suffer from a bad attack of 'Inversion-itis.'

As we started to ascend the hill a strange phenomenon began to show itself. An inversion! This was the first time I had ever seen one. Fundamentally the upper air keeps the cloud and bad weather low in the valleys. The overcast, bleak conditions in the village belied the weather on the mountain. As we approached the car park we emerged through the cloud to be greeted by a crystal clear sky.

It turned out to be one off the best days of the season. Aviemore at it's best. So many people had been fooled into not skiing (not just Ben and his lot) that the lifts had no lines. No waiting and great snow.

The view was amazing. It was like being on an island looking over a sea of clouds. Absolutely stunning. What a day.

We got back down Ben had gone into hiding! Not from us I hasten to add, but he had some explaining to do to his group. Poor guy had a lot of schmoozing to do that night. And the true friends that we were...we thought it was a hoot and laughed our socks off.

Ah it's great to have Pals!

"What size o' skis d'ye want Jeannie?"

Over the years I've seen people do strange things. When I worked in the Colorado ski area of Beaver Creek I met two couples who were on vacation together. One pair were beginners and I was going to teach them for the day. The other pair were, as the girl put it, 'experts'. Could I show them which expert runs that I'd recommend. No problem. Actually Beaver Creek is pretty straight forward as most of the more challenging runs are on 'Grouse Mountain.' Although this is within the area and is easy to get to; it can only be accessed by it's own chairlift. This is good as no unsuspecting novice can meander on to it by mistake.) I dutifully pointed out on the map how to get there and off they went.

The morning went well. Another great day in my office. We were soon buzzing around the hill and lunch came in a blink of an eye. We were sitting enjoying a well earned beer when the other two arrived to join us for lunch. Through the meal we listened to all the derring-do's that the other couple had been up to on the scary Grouse Mountain. Where they had obviously been having a ball all morning.

As we were getting ready to leave one of the experts told me that her boots were giving her some pain. Could I suggest something that would help. Of course I could, if she'd show me where they hurt. Not a problem and at that she stood up to show where she was getting pain....so with her boyfriend, the other couple and quite a few of the other diners in the restaurant looking on, I had to explain that she had her boots on the wrong feet...Oops!

However I think that the best happened in dear old Aviemore.

Windy conditions would regularly force us to hold beginner classes other than on the hill. First choice would be the 'Hay Field.' This was an area just after Loch Morlich. Actually it was an ideal place for beginners. It was sheltered with a nice gentle slope. It would have been the place for beginners even when the weather was good.

Another alternative for beginners was on the front lawn of the Strathspey Hotel. As it is in full view from the main road it was a good marketing ploy too. On this lawn I was to witness a 'duzie.'

In effect the lawn was another great place for beginners. Regularly we'd have dozens of classes going on. Everybody got a chance to laugh at the people in the other groups as well as their own. This helped create a great atmosphere.

All morning there had been something that had been niggling at the back of my mind . You know when you see something and your brain nags at you....there is something wrong with this picture. You don't see what it is but....

Then, well into the afternoon session the penny dropped.
This lovely lady from Inverness area. She'd be in her late fifties and was having a great time. She also had these beautifully lacquered wooden skis. I was admiring them, when it suddenly hit me....I finally saw what I had been unconsciously aware of all day...half of the back of her skis was missing!

"What happened to your skis?" I asked incredulously.

"Oh that was my husband." She replied with that lovely lilt that Gaelic speakers have.

"He had heard that short skis were all the rage now. So he took them into the shed and cut them down to size for me."

There she was, happy as Larry...on these mutilated skis!!!
She looked like an extra out of Kizmet!

JEANNIE. WHAT LENGTH DO YOU WANT THESE SKIS TO BE?

For one of the few times in my life,
I was speechless.

THE LONDONER

The first winter I worked in the Alps coincided with the opening of a British bar called "The Londoner." The owners already had a Londoner Bar in Kitzbuhel and had decided to open a new bar in our area. As I was the only Brit who worked for the ski school I had been invited to the opening.

A group of us turned up and at the door. I was introduced to the owners. A nice couple of guys.

"Are you Les?"

"Yeah."

"Well your drinks are free." I was told.

I liked this conversation...it was to get better because they didn't mean free drinks just for the opening night...they meant free for the season!!

I immediately started looking around for people playing harps. I thought I'd died and gone to heaven. Nope, no Cherubs hanging around...no one stoking a big fire either.

I promptly introduced my buddy Mark, an American from Oregon, to them and he was granted the same status.

This had the makings of a great season.

Mark was one of two Yanks who had got a job with the ski school. Talk about a small world. Both came from the same State but they had never met. Also they were as different as you could get. Mark was a big city guy and the other, a really nice kid, was just off the ranch. He was a real 'Howdy Doody.'

Can you imagine, they lived 60 miles apart in Oregon and met up in a little Austrian town a few thousand miles away? Talk about degrees of separation.

It got weirder.

Mark had told me about how, when he was a teenager, he used to ski around with an old WWI German helmet on. Around the beginning of February we were all sitting around when our young 'Howdy' talked about how he used to watch this crazy skier back on Mount Hood. This guy he said was a lunatic doing summersaults and all sorts in the bumps...I used do them too-but everyone recognised them as falls, spectacular, but falls. This guy however actually **meant** to do them we were assured.

"Yeah this maniac used to ski down wearing an old German helmet."
Mark and I looked at each other and burst out laughing. Small world eh?

The bar staff were made up of mainly Aussies, Kiwis and

Canucks. They were doing the return to the old country on a working holiday thing.

It was a great milieu to be in. They'd come over for a year or two. Work in London (Earl's Court was dubbed 'Kangaroo Court' at that time) Using the UK as a base they'd do all sorts of trips around Europe.

They also had a wonderful network of jobs world wide. I got in on it and had offers to work in Darwin should I decided to go overland to Australia. I nearly went to work at a ski school in Tehran because of it. I did end up working for a company guiding treks across Africa through it. Oh the job network was a great thing to get in on and that was how most of the bar staff came to be in Austria.

That the Londoner was a success in Kitzbuhel was obvious by the extraordinary measure the locals went to trying to get it closed down. At one point they sat outside the Londoner in Kitzbuhel with decibel counters! To 'counter' this there was a guy at the door to usher clients in and out via two heavy, (very heavy) curtains. Closing one before opening the other in an attempt to stop the bedlam from within escaping to the waiting Austrians and their sonic detectors.

It was akin to going into a 'Speak Easy' from prohibition days. I think I saw Elliot Ness drinking in a corner....but then again that might have been the effect of free drinks!

Of course this added to the reputation of the bar. It was like my old army days. Arrive at a new posting...read 'Orders' to find out which bars were 'Off Limits' et voila, you had your list of preferred watering holes.

Through the winter he owners were true to their word I never paid for a drink the whole time I was there. Later in the season I asked them about it and they explained that any group that I had would ask me what was a good place to go for a drink. I would honestly say that I always drank at the Londoner. So I would get my first drink from the pub but then my group would arrive and buy the rest. My first gig in marketing!. For the rest of the winter I did as much 'marketing' as my liver could stand.

Thus my first season in The Alps passed in a haze.

NEW YEARS EVE

St.Johann was gearing up for New Years Eve. All the instructors were to be involved in the ski school display.

Mark and I were into freestyle skiing. This was in its embryo stage. Nothing like what these guys do now but it was fun being in at the start. At that time Austria was very traditional in their approach. Ski teachers weren't supposed to be jumping and falling about. Our behaviour on the slopes was frowned on by the old guard. I guess we came across as wild men. However we were included in the 'Jump Team' for the upcoming New Year Show.

For a week or so we had been practicing on the jump that had been built at the base of the mountain. There were six of us and the idea was that we'd go one after another. Not with a gap between each jumper but like a stick of Paratroopers exiting a plane, it was...Go,Go,Go!

Practices went great. I was second from last and Mark brought up the rear. We were to do two jumps the first one was through a hoop. The second was just a straight forward one with no hoop and we could do whatever kind of jump we wanted. No problem...a piece o' cake right?

Comes the day. All the ski school, instructors, office workers friends et al, collect and we head up on the mountain tram to a Gasthof on the hill. The spectacle was to start at around 7.00pm so we had plenty of time to kill.

Everything started of nicely then we got to the toasts. First the owner of the Gasthof. A wee speech followed by Schnapps all round and with a "Prosit!" We downed the schnapps. There was then, what seemed to be, an endless procession of the hierarchy each wishing us well in the coming season followed by another schnapps and...Prosit!

After many,many,many...Prosits we went to get our skis on. As you can imagine by the time came to ski down there weren't too many sober skiers. Picture the scene as a multitude of 'tipsy' skiers attempt to line up in the dark. Then we were given these flare like candles. Drunks, on skis and armed with flaming torches...Health and Safety...eat your hearts out.

We were positioned in two lines and the plan was that we were to converge and separate all the way down. And thus; drunk, on skis, in the dark and wielding a flaming torch, we set off.

I was informed later that it looked great as the people watched enthralled watching these two glowing lines snake their way down the slope.

All I can say is that the unseen mayhem that ensued en route was hilarious. Skiers colliding or shooting off into the trees only to reappear covered in twigs and pines shouting for someone to reignite their torch. The biggest hazard was, of course, getting skewered by another skiers flaming torch. I can assure you that quite a few left with singed bums, grace of the following skier.

Surviving the descent we made our way over to the run in for the jump. Looking down at the jump the hoop looked pretty small especially as it was now belching flames. It was on fire! At least we had plenty of light so off we shot. We were in a nice tight formation. As we approached the burning hoop everything was going fine then as I passed through the flames I heard

"Scheiße!!"

Someone had fallen, I heard the cry just as I had passed through the hoop. At the same time I discovered that I had lost my night vision. I was momentarily blind. Never thought of that did we? Of course the flames would blind us at night...Duh!?

So there I was waiting for my vision to clear, hurtling to the ground like a mortar shell. Not a lot of fun, especially as I didn't know if someone was lying prostrate on the ground beneath and acutely aware that there was another kamikaze right behind me. And he was a BIG, BRAWNY, SIX FOOT KAMIKAZE!!!

One of those "Oh shit!" moments.

Fortunately I landed without a mishap.

We all clambered back up the slope to the ramp for our second jump. Thankfully there would be no flaming hoop this time. We had all sobered up somewhat since the last jump. Amazing what a wee scare will do.

As we prepared they set fire to the wood that had been piled at the base of the jump. This time we had to go through a wall of flame. With the adrenalin pumping we set off. This time I knew about the loss of vision caused by going from the bright flame to the darkness of the other side so I kept one eye closed for the run in.

As we reached the run-in someone decided that the wall of flame wasn't 'wall' enough and threw some more fuel onto the bonfire just as we took air.

There was a thunderous WHOOMP! as we passed through the wall of fire, singeing our eyebrows, hair, gloves and ski suits all at the same time.

Who said we guys can't multi task!

THE KIDS GROUP
<u>And it's aftermath.</u>

One of the perceived punishments meted out by the boss of the ski school was to be 'demoted' to taking a kids group. So after one of my many misdemeanours I was given a kids group for the week.

It was to be one of the 'Funner' (I got that word from my 'Howdy Doody' pal from Oregon.) and harrowing weeks that I was to have.

Firstly, Kids, you've got to watch them like hawks. Take your eye off them and they can (and will) disappear off into the wild blue yonder. It became standard modus operandi to stop and count the little tykes every 100 metres or so.

I had organized the kids to shout out 'Wipe Out!' if anyone in the group was to fall so we could all come to a screeching halt. The immediate effect of me stopping was for the first two kids to ski straight into me. They thought this was great fun so from then on every time I stopped they used me as their preferred method of stopping. Every stop would result in a...Bump,bump followed by a fit of giggles.

Halfway through the week we'd had a fresh snow fall and the snow at the edge of the runs was soft and deep.

As we were skiing down one of the kids missed a turn and shot off into the deeper snow and went ace over base...a few times!

"WIPE OUT!!" Rang out from the kids, followed by BaBump! Looking round I saw the poor kid lying in the deep snow some 30 feet back up the hill. Now when kids fall their bodies can adopt some amazing twists and positions added to that they bawl like banshees. Looking at the tangled mess I was sure he had broken something as he looked like a knot a sailor would have been proud off. Quick as a flash I had my skis off and was running back up the slope.

Looking down on this squealing kid, who was now shaped like a pretzel, I tried to figure out how to untie the 'grannie knot' he'd got himself into. I gently untangled the poor lad and stood him back on his feet. He immediately stopped screeching and shot off down to join the others as if nothing had happened.

Sweating and panting after my exertions (but very relieved that the little tyke wasn't injured) I looked down at my little angels who were now a happy smiling bunch and before I could say or do anything they burst out into their another of their preferred chants.

"Immer Weiter...Immer Weiter!" (Basically...why are we waiting!)
Oh they thought it had been great fun watching me run up the hill in a panic! You can rest assured that, much to

their amusement, the 'joke' was to be repeated many times during the week.

Kid's group in ATTACK FORMATION

A few years later I was to see another take on this wheeze. It was in Beaver Creek, Colorado. My pupil and I had just arrived at the bottom after a great days skiing when we saw the ski patrol sled coming down the hill. In the back there was an adult, who was clearly the injured party, all wrapped up and in some discomfort. He must have been skiing with his kids as the ski patrol had sat them in the sled beside him bringing them down together.

There they were, these two kids (about seven years old) Bouncing, smiling and giggling generally having a whale of a time zooming down in the 'blood wagon' completely oblivious to the grimacing adult that they were using as a cushion.

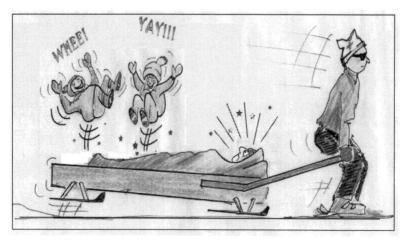

I can just imagine them the following year...
" Can we do it again Dad....Huh...huh....
Can we..can we?"

Happily we all survived the week. There was the usual little ceremony for the kids. I had written out their certificates and handed out their medals. The two wee girls that had been skiing into me as their preferred method of stopping presented me with a with a little wooden heart (I've still got it) and gave me hug. (Y' can't beat it.)

Then it was the parents turn. (About 15 of them.) Unfortunately most of them were leaving right away and insisted (individually) that I must have a Schnapps and a Prosit! Consequently I downed a lot of Schnapps in a very short time. At some point I had gone to the bathroom and had promptly fallen asleep on the throne.

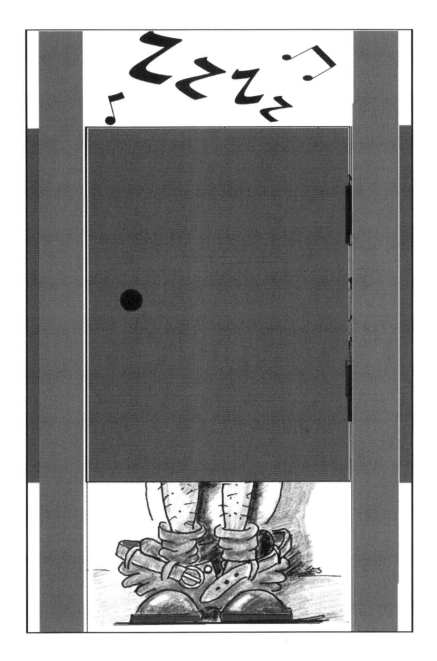

Waking a few hours later I found that I was awake....but my legs weren't. AARGH!
After suffering the agonies of 'pins and needles and still

trying desperately to get my legs to function properly. I returned - moving with a weird gate that comes from not really feeling your legs - back into the bar and was immediately met with a huge cheer. The other instructors had been waiting for me to emerge and have a good laugh at my expense.

They got their moment.

THE HOUSE THAT MOVED

A lot of my stories originate from Aviemore in Scotland... you may have noticed; I make no apologies for that. During the late seventies into the early eighties Aviemore was an incredible place with more characters to the square inch than anywhere else I have worked.

Package skiing holidays to the Alps were still in their infancy and people thought that it would be good to get their first taste of skiing in their own country. They came from all over the U.K. and consequently Aviemore was brimming over with tourists. It was its golden era.

There was even a group called 'The weekend ski club' that bussed people all the way up from London and it's surrounding area for the weekend. They would arrive on the Saturday morning, ski all-day and party like there was no tomorrow in the evening. Some of them actually made the ski slopes on the Sunday, but not a few made their way to the bar in search of the hair of the dog.

On the Sunday evening they would all be herded into the buses and wend their way back to the 'Smoke' in time for work on the Monday morning. What the atmosphere on the bus was like I wouldn't care to imagine, teeming with bodies, either 'freshly(?)' liberated from their ski togs after a days skiing or inebriated souls surgically removed from the bar. A wonderful combination to be enclosed in a bus for a twelve hour trip. I can't think of a more refreshing way to spend a Sunday! God knows what their Bosses thought when they encountered them first thing the following morning

With the resort brimming and taking into account the attitudes of the era it was no wonder that things got a wee bit wild. Some say that we instructors did more than our fair share to contribute to the state of affairs, certainly it was difficult to stay out of the holiday spirit and having our changing room next door to the "Illicit Still" bar wasn't a help either.

We would come straight down from the slopes, take off our boots and Bee-line it to the bar.
If the ambience was good - as it usually was - a quick beer would turn into an evening session.

Tuesday and Thursday nights were especially dangerous as after closing time.

This was a quaint thing we had in that the bars in Scotland would close at Ten in the evening. Ten minutes before closing they would shout

"Last Orders!"

This cry would be met by a charge to the bar that would out-do the Light Brigade's tilt at the Russian guns at Balaclava, everyone, well ok, the guys, would order two or three drinks just for themselves, these they would attempt to quaff down in the remaining time before getting chucked out.

Consequently there was definite peak to the evening where everyone arrived in the same state at the same time. The bar would re-open half an hour later as a Disco Club and we could continue until one in the morning.

During this half-hour hiatus most of us would repair to the White Lady Bar, so we wouldn't go thirsty. This nice bar was situated on the next floor so there wasn't too much break in the continuity of the evening.

On one of these Disco evenings a friend and I made the acquaintance of two charming young ladies who graciously accepted our invitation to a late night cup of cocoa 'Chez nous'.

At the time we were living in a mobile home, it was called "Damn-one." (Which is another story) The house was situated in the centre of the village, but tonight it's title of mobile home would be well earned. As we arrived at our destination, we discovered that it wasn't, our destination that is, well it should have been, but as our goal was our house it was a case of we were there but the house didn't show! There we were, one thirty in the morning, not exactly in the soberest of states trying to convince two girls that...

"Honest the house was here this morning."

Needless to say it wasn't long before we were on our own, the ladies, coming to their senses had shot off home leaving us to stagger around looking for our house. It took about half an hour to find the bloody thing!

Workmen, who were in the process of building a new block had actually moved the damn thing round the corner, some five hundred yards away and out of sight and no b****r thought to tell us!

CAUGHT SHORT!!!

This story is apocryphal as I've heard a version of it in every country that I have worked in but it is worth the space.

Toilets, or rather the lack of them has always been a problem for skiers, especially those of the fairer sex, putting a bit of a dent in the idea that god might be a woman. This is the story of an unfortunate woman who finds herself on top of a mountain with nowhere to go.

After warming up with a few glasses of hot wine the young lady got the chairlift for the top. She realised that there are consequences of drinking then going out into the cold, but there was no real problem as it wasn't one of the longer lifts there was plenty of time to go up and ski back down. A dull ache in the bladder was not something that was too much of a concern as she sat down and relaxed on the chairlift. What is it they say about the best-laid plans of mice and men?

Well, of course when things shouldn't go wrong 'Sods law' dictates that they will. Sure enough about a third of the way up.... The lift broke down. Our poor lass started to get uncomfortable.

Five minutes waiting turned into ten, to twenty, finally just before fifty minutes had passed the lift burst into life, fortunately before a part of her anatomy followed suit. How did she know how much time had passed...?

Believe me anyone in that situation knows the passing of every torturous minute. By the time she had reached the top she had crossed her legs, arms, eyes any part of her body that could be crossed, was. Her main hope was her crossed fingers- well it's difficult to ski crossed legged. On alighting from the chairlift she realise that she didn't have a snowball in hells chance of making it back down to the bar and the haven of its toilets.

Frantically she scoured the immediate vicinity, the only thing around to save her from the gaze of the skiers milling around was a rocky outcrop. Off she shot into the lee of the rocks. Of course getting there was only part of the battle; it was now a struggle against time to divest herself of her ski gear, zips, buttons, clips all of which seemed to conspire against her. Finally she managed to free herself enough to be able to squat down and sigh with the relief.

Squatting there she thought her ordeal was over, but oh no her problems were about to get worse.... Much worse. Using the maxim of undo or take off only that which is required to complete the necessary function she had concluded, correctly, that the removal of her skis was not something required especially as her situation needed speed. There she was revelling in the ecstasy of relief, eyes closed, savouring the moment.

Gradually a new sensation started to gain ground...just as her skis were. She opened her eyes like a startled deer to see, to her dismay, her worst fears confirmed, she was indeed starting to slide down the hill.

The motion of her squatting had given momentum to the skis, and with the certainty of a train pulling away from a platform she was gathering speed. Any skier, which means most if not all of us, knows that sitting on the backs of the skis is not the ideal position to control the skis let alone their speed.

Now she had a bigger dilemma, did she stand up, pull her pants up and stop her forward progress, or should she fall to one side using her bum as a brake? She of course took another option... she panicked.

As it was it is doubtful if she could have stemmed the flow that was now in full flood. So leaving a trail of yellow snow behind her she continued her gently accelerating decent of the slope managing to slide her way through an open mouthed ski class. Burying her head in her hands she meandered her way down until at last the flow stopped.

Hastily she pulled up her pants and skied off faster than she thought possible

She was never seen again.

PLUM

Aviemore was full of characters and this next tale involves one of the more prominent. Plum came from the north of England and was, depending upon whom you spoke to either a dullard or phlegmatic, one of the things that most agreed on was that he was definitely one of the better plumbers around.

Plum was one of these guys that seem to have been born looking old. The one good thing about that is that everyone else catches up. I first met him in the seventies and when I saw him about twenty years later and he looked exactly the same, I of course looked every inch of the twenty years older.

Anyone who has worked with him can attest to his high pain threshold. One day as he was hammering some nails into a beam he inadvertently belted his thumb with an almighty whack. Grown men beside him were being sick or fainting, not Plum he simply substituted his thumb for his pipe, sucked on it for a few seconds and uttered

"Ee' tha' nipped a bit."

One evening while having an after ski drink in one of Aviemore's more frequented watering holes the legendary Winking Owl. There was the usual throng jamming the bar and Plum got into conversation with one of the local ski teachers. (I think it was Hughie.)

"Know what lad? " He said to the half-interested instructor.

"T'day for the first time my boots gave me jip."

This last phrase grabbed the attention of his previously inattentive listener. People in the bar also started to take an interest and there was a lull in the bar conversations, well Plum and pain were not exactly synonymous. People were still chatting on but one ear was tuning into Plums words and as he continued there was a definite quietening of the usually raucous crowd. It wasn't a conscious thing just involuntary ear-wigging

"Now these boots have never given me trouble before," he droned on oblivious to his ever-increasing audience.

"T'day they gave me a real pressure point right here." he said pointing to the appropriate area of his little toe.

"Well y'know when I got down off the hill and took m'boot off d'y know wot I found? "

By now an audible silence hung over the bar as he reached down and rummaged in his bag straightening he held up his hand.

"Look at that, it was in my boot..."

All eyes focused in on his outstretched hand...a

sparkplug!!

He had been skiing all day with
a car's sparkplug in his ski boot.
The bar died.

THE LIFT OF THE DEAD

I heard this next one from some pupils so I can't confirm personally to its authenticity however it is such a great practical joke it *should* be true.

A group of guys were having a great holiday in Tignes France, terrific skiing and good partying. Despite the evening's revelry it was a matter of honour that they appear for the first lift in the morning. No matter how 'Hung over' they were or indeed if they were still inebriated, their attendance was a matter of honour they could then happily go and die in some corner if they wished, but being there was the order of the day.

At first the 'lifties' were a bit disgruntled with the 'Bloody English' but as the week progressed they got used to seeing the madmen waiting to get the first gondola.

As we know familiarity breeds contempt and as their holiday progressed the lift attendants took less and less notice of the group. At last the final day of their holiday came around and they set their plan into action.

Using, the now, less than vigilant attitude of the French four of the group slipped onto one of the gondolas just before opening time, while the lift was still in the testing phase prior to opening to the public. On the journey up one of them produced a couple of packets of baking flour and they proceeded to sprinkle the flour over themselves.

When the gondola arrived at the top station they were well doused in this powder giving an ethereal image. As their cabin pulled into the station the poor unsuspecting lift attendants were first puzzled to see figures already in a cabin, puzzlement grew as the figures not only made no attempt to get out of the gondola...they didn't move at all!

The cabin made it's way along the station drawing closer to where the 'lifties' were participating in a quiet little breakfast prior to the hoards of skiers arriving. Curiosity was starting to change into concern as the figures got closer and they got a clearer view of the occupants.

The flour had given a the group a ghostly look. Concern was quickly replaced with panic as the 'lifties' came to the conclusion that these must be people frozen to death after spending the night stuck on the lift, something not unheard of in ski resorts.

That was it the proverbial **** hit the fan. Buzzers went off, phones turned red hot, ambulances raced to the scene, and Police were called.

The 'lifties' were having apoplexy. Worse was to follow, as the attendants rushed out to the cabin the 'Dead bodies' suddenly came to life almost giving the poor

Frenchmen heart attacks, that no one actually had a coronary speaks wonders for a glass of the ol' vin rouge for breakfast.

It didn't take long for the pranksters to realise the lift operators were not quite as amused with their joke as they themselves were. Managing to get their skis on before the French gathered their wits they skied off down the hill.

At the bottom luck was with them as they just managed to evade the waiting Police and some very angry and agitated Frenchmen.

Fortunately it was the lads last day in resort otherwise their well being could be said to have been in jeopardy. As it was they were lucky to escape Tignes with their wedding tackle still attached to their bodies.

QUEUE JUMPING

One of the best practical jokes I've ever known to be played on skiers happened in my own country of Scotland. In the late seventies and early eighties the ski area of Aviemore was an extremely busy place.

The lift-lines were notoriously long at the busy periods as indeed it still is today at the weekends. Most of the time the lines were orderly and were, in the main, self regulated, something that would appear to be very Anglo Saxon, as anyone has survived the battle of the Continental lift line can attest. There are always some people who consider waiting in line is for lesser mortals other than themselves.

At the bottom of one of the main runs, "The White Lady," the lift operators that worked the T-Bar lifts serving the run were getting fed up getting their ears bent by people complaining about queue jumpers. One evening after a few liquid refreshments two of them hatched the following plan...

The following weekend was its usual chock-a-block self. The slopes were teeming with skiers, queues were taking up to and over half an hour to clear. Waiting until their lift's queue had reached its peak their plan unfolded.
A 'skier' appeared and started, in a somewhat unsubtle way, jostling his way through the lift line drawing the ire of many a skier. Arriving at the front of the line he

was confronted by his mate the lift operator. There started the altercation, acted out in front of an appreciative, if somewhat captivated, waiting audience.

"I've told you a hundred times not to jump the queue." bellowed the irate attendant.

This was followed by the typical 'argie-bargie' of men puffing themselves up for a fight, quite enthralling the crowd around them. Suddenly our intrepid lift operator broke off with a cry of...

" I'll fix you, You b..."

The last word was lost on the crowd as he disappeared into the lift hut. The issue hung in the air until the attendant stormed out of the hut brandishing a bloody great axe. With a cry of "Gotcha ya bas!" He proceeded to hack the errant line jumper's skis to smithereens.

The stunned silence from the lift line was palpable; much shuffling immediately followed it, as everyone made sure that they were not perceived as 'Pushing in' by the obviously unglued lift attendant.

When the hapless skier finally traipsed off with his shattered skis he left behind lift lines that would have done a regiment of guards proud.

OKAY...Who's next?

Needless to say there was no further problems with queue jumping that day.

FASHION BEFORE THE FALL

It had been a beautiful day of spring skiing in perfect conditions. The sun had been shining all day and we had been skiing nice big soft bumps. It had been really hot everyone was in sweaters or `T´ - shirts, we even had a streaker ski the main run! Unfortunately, for us, it was a guy...but that's another story but you can still buy the post card!

An instructor and I had stopped skiing just before a stretch of bumps at a run called the "gun barrel." It isn't particularly steep or even long, but because of its shape it usually has great bumps and as it is at the bottom of the slopes it makes an ideal 'end of the day' run.

We had been hammering our legs in the bumps quite a bit during the afternoon and were resting a moment to get our wind back. We also wanted to let the area clear a bit of all the people then we could blitz down the middle, a perfect end to the day.

We had adopted the ski teacher pose, looking in on the run and leaning on our poles. With our mirrored glasses on we could check out all the pretty 'Ladies' skiing around in their stretch pants, without them really being sure if we were actually looking at them or not - Great inventions, mirrored glasses, ideal for the surreptitious letch.

A girl I know told me this joke...

"Why do ski instructors wear mirrored sunglasses?"

"So they can see themselves when they talk to each other!"

Which I thought was a great send up, I of course never wear mirrored sunglasses...Now.

There was a particularly attractive girl wending her way down towards us. Both of our radar had picked her up from some distance away, probably something to do with the way she filled her stretch pants and sweater.

She really did look the part with her long flowing blond hair framed by the blue cloudless sky. No one would of course known for sure that we were looking in her direction as we studiously kept our head at almost ninety degrees to her while cranking our eyes over to the max.

As she drew closer to us she must have caught an edge, or a 'Snow snake' grabbed her ankle or something of the like and over she went. Now most times when people fall it's a simple tip over to the side or a sedate parking of the bum on the snow, however there are times when the word spectacular is just not adequate, this was one of them. It was a beaut.

Over she went in a flurry of poles, snow, skis,

sunglasses, limbs and blond hair, finally coming to rest almost directly opposite us. She landed on her back with her arms and legs stretched out in a star shape with her legs and feet towards us. The heels of her skis had buried themselves up to the bindings in the deep spring snow, which by this time of the day had reached the consistency of porridge...being a Scot I know about these things.

As with all falls of this kind they are followed by a moment of getting in contact with the nether regions checking that they are still functioning. Starting at the toes you usually work your way up through the other movable parts. When satisfied all is as should be we start to get up. This is when our young lady started to realise she had a problem, the heels of her skis were stuck fast and she started doing an impersonation of a beetle trying to get off it's back. She struggled and struggled to no avail, she was stuck.

Like the true gentlemen that we were we immediately went over to help and as we went to haul her skis out of the snow all three of us noticed something that was going to add considerably to the young lady's discomfort...

Slowly there came a dawning that something wasn't quite right with the picture that rested before us.
She must have had that awareness, something akin to the moment Colonel Custer said,

"Oh s**t!" as he saw all the Indians that were coming across the Little Big Horn river.

Simultaneously all three of us recognised her faux pas.... She had split the inside seam of the leg stitching of her stretch pants. It had split from one knee all the way over to her other knee. This would have been bad enough but this unfortunate girl had obviously decided that panties weren't going to destroy the line of her pants. I don't know which was faster, her hands reaching down to cover her...well to cover her, or the colour of her face going from pure white to an amazing colour of red. Warp speed comes to mind. She probably wished Scotty could have beamed her up too!

I can only imagine what was going through her mind as we prised the heels of her skis loose from the snow while she determinedly held on to her crotch. Once up she gave us a flustered thank you and shot off.

The poor girls torment wasn't over. Once we got down to the village we repaired to our usual watering hole " The Illicit Still Bar" and proceeded to recount the event to the other instructors.

We were of course met with howls of "Bull**it.... Tell us another...Pull the other.... Etc.
Almost on cue, the girl walked into the bar with her boyfriend. She was facing away from our table and hadn't spotted us.

There we were pointing over at her when the poor lass chose that moment to turn around and survey the bar only to be confronted by some fifteen ski teachers staring in her direction and the two of us pointing.

An involuntary noise escaped her lips and her face did its amazing colouring trick again then she turned on her heels and shot out of the bar followed by a bewildered boyfriend and us...we sympathetic souls?
We were in hysterics.

There is a moral to this tale. Your mother would say "Don't go out without clean underwear...well

"DON'T GO WITHOUT!"

HOOKY BOBBING

I was lucky enough to work in an Austrian Ski School at the same time as a guy called Mark. He was from Oregon, a shade under six feet, a great skier and very good looking. Of this luck of birth he didn't seem to be the least bit conscious, nor of the fact that women were drooling over him.

He was a great character and we had great fun during the season. He was among the best skiers that I've had the privilege to ski with. He was also a bit off a 'nutter' on skis. Always looking to get as much air from any bump, lump or lip that he could jump from. He even had a T-shirt with the slogan more air more hair, which, as I still had mine at the time, I thought was quite cool.

We tore around the mountain like a couple of Kamikazes much to the chagrin of the Ski School bosses. They were of the old school and us tearing up the mountain in our time off, well 'alles vas nicht in ordnung.' In Austria ski instructors were not supposed to fall, and having fun on the slopes was not considered in keeping with the image.
Shades of 'Vee haff vays of teaching you to ski...You vill not enjoy zem.

Did we care...Nah.
On one slope Mark spotted what looked like a possible jump, a lip way, way down the slope. After pointing it out

he took off like a Bat out of Hell. As soon as I saw where he was going off I went after him. It was a nice shaped lip but we couldn't see exactly where it led to. But it was going away from the slope that we were on so there was no chance of hitting another skier.

We blazed in at the lip both in the downhill racers tuck, we wanted to get up high so we needed the speed. He hit the lip and I watched him go up, up, up. God was he going up.

As I came into the jump he was in a beautiful 'Back Scratcher' and skis crossed as he dropped down and out of sight. It was at about the time of him disappearing that I had my first thoughts of
"What's on the other side?"

Too late I was on the run-in. I extended my legs with all my force to get as much lift as I could. Boy did I fly. Opening out into a 'Spread-eagle' I looked down through my skis and found out what was on the other side. Mark was. Him and his equipment were strewn all over the landing site looking for all the world like a Garage Sale.

There he was sprawled in the deep snow wetting himself laughing- later he said it was because of the look on my face. Look on my face, I'll bet it was strange and can you blame me when I'm way up in the air and having run out off steam was starting to drop to earth like a second world war V1 rocket over London, and what do I see before me...a bloody driveway. We were only trying to cross one of the ubiquitous GastHoff's drive cum car park.

We had, by luck, managed to be passing between two cars. However the bank of snow that had been created by the Snow Plough was just high enough, or we were just low enough that Mark had clipped it and had gone 'A over T' into the snow. And me, well I was still waiting for gravity to hurl me to the same fate, which it did. Crash! There I was having my own Garage Sale.

I emerged from the deep snow with most of the white stuff in places it really shouldn't have been. We looked at each other and had a fit off the giggles. We were stopped by a sudden gruff voice barking at us, we looked around and saw that the whole episode had been seen by half of the Ski School. They had watched it all unfold from the lofty perch of a chairlift.

Unfortunately it was the half that contained the Boss who was having a fit of his own. He was obviously an unhappy chappy and was screaming something at us, but it was in German so we didn't understand, ergo didn't care. Whatever it was he was certainly going to have a hard time with his blood pressure. The colour his face was turning, well if he'd been walking along the street he would have stopped all the traffic. This had the unfortunate effect seen in one of Peter Sellers famous 'Out-takes' and we went into uncontrollable laughter. We laughed so hard the tears ran down our legs.

When we arrived that evening at the Ski School we were meted out the inevitable punishment. All us 'Auslanders' were to be banished to a Chalet at the other end off town. Normally all the Ski Teachers were housed in the Ski Lehrer Heim a building right next to the Ski School, which meant rolling out of bed and into work. Now we had a walk of about half an hour. As one of the lads said

"If we were any further we'd need our bloody passports."

A slight exaggeration but you get the idea.

There we were two Yanks a Canuck and myself and, before I forget, my long-suffering girlfriend. She was there quite surreptitiously having been banned by the Boss who was miffed that she had taken a job as a secretary and not worked for his Ski School. He suspected that she was there but could never quite catch her. Little did he realise that this 'Banishment' was going to prove to be even more of an embarrassment for him.

Mark introduced me to what he called 'Hookie Bobbing'. He swore blind that he and his mates back in Oregon used this mode of transport all the time in winter. Now kiddies this is a definite "Do not try this at home" job.

This is a winter only affair and requires snow-covered roads. Standing by a set of traffic lights or crossroads and looking as innocent as you possibly can wait until you see a car that is going in the desired direction. Quickly move in behind the car and squat down holding onto the fender/bumper.

Two points to ponder, make sure the roads have not been gritted- unless you're addicted to getting the occasional rub down by sandpaper and never ever pick the side with the exhaust! When the car pulls off you go with it. Simple. If it signals or starts to head in a direction that you don't want, let go, you'll glide to a stop and then repeat the whole thing with another car. Voila you've just helped cut down on congestion in the inner Cities.

For the next few weeks this was our 'modus operandi' to and from work. We were driving the local Police and motorists nuts. The Cops couldn't see us until we had passed and the look on driver's faces when we'd appear some distance from where they had last seen us was priceless. You could see bewilderment in their eyes. They were sure they had seen us a few blocks back but there we were again. Doctors were probably disturbed by the sudden outbreak of Deja Vu in the Town. Wearing our Ski School uniforms was probably a give away but then again nobody could actually catch us in the act. So...

"Who us?" Said as innocently as possible was the order of the day.

Our new abode, apart from being so far away was also a bit on the cold side. It had an old wood boiler, a small, a very small wood boiler in the basement. We got fed up with tepid baths and cold bedrooms. We were working outside in sub zero temperature all day and we needed to reheat our bodies in the evenings. Hypothermia is accumulative that is to say that if you get really cold one day and don't get a chance to reheat you're core temperature, the next day you're starting one step closer to getting Hypothermia.

It came to a head during the busy February period when we were spending upwards of six hours out in sub zero conditions. We decided we had had enough so taking it in relays, we stoked the boiler for all it was worth. We had it going great guns. The pipes were rattling away good style. Steam was coming out of the faucets. It was like living in a sauna. It was warm. There was none of the usual dashing to get under the bedcovers before the onset of frostbite. it was wonderful. But we were going through the wood at an alarming rate. After a couple of days we had to go and ask for more wood, move over Oliver Twist.

More wood...More Wood?!

You'd have thought we'd asked him to cut his leg off. It would appear that we had used what was normally a month's supply in under a week. Oh dearie me. He obviously couldn't believe that we had used that amount of wood in so short a time and gave us a surprise visit that evening.

Using his own key he stormed into the house. My girlfriend, Catherine had just come out of the bath and wrapped in only a small towel just managed to hide in my room. He came into the living room just as the heating system was rendering a sound not unlike the crescendo of the 1812 Overture. He went ballistic.

We were moved to a brand new Chalet right next to the lift. The following week, strangely enough, the Deja Vu phenomenon that had cursed the Town was also over.

STRANGE PLACES

Have you ever noticed that when going up a chairlift how often you see people in the oddest places? Going through the trees or on a vast flat plateau and for the life of you can never figure out how they got there, what the are going to do now that they've got there and more importantly...Why!?

I've seen something similar in Africa. A few years ago I led a trek across the Sahara and every now and then we'd see this lone figure wandering out of the desert coming from seemingly nowhere and going nowhere. We'd pour over our maps but still couldn't figure out where the buggers were coming *from* never mind where they were going to. Was there a party and nobody had invited us?

These people are alive and well and now bugging the hell out of me in ski resorts, where are they going? What do they know that I don't? I can never get close to them to ask. I've tried shouting from the lift but they just smile, wave and wander off. Is it a Scott of the Antarctic thing or what!

During my career I've been fortunate enough to be able to teach quite a lot of off-trail deep snow skiing. The big mountains of the French Alps have given me some memorable days, this was to be one of them. I had a couple that were good skiers and we had spent the afternoon, in the words of Captain Kirk, going where no man has gone before, in the hunt for fresh untracked snow.

It was coming towards the end of the day and we dropped down and into an obscure bowl. There was a trail but it passed at ninety degrees to us and was a lot higher than where we were. It was in pristine condition, being far enough out of the way to have been left untouched all day. We were delighted. A traverse across to where I knew the snow would be the deepest moved us to within some 25 yards of a little ledge that several trees were clinging to. I set about explaining the route that they were to follow and was in the process of explaining technique, as we teachers are apt to do, when we heard a strange cry.

We looked at each other, shook our heads, nah it couldn't have been, and we continued with the lesson. Then we heard it again more distinct, it was a definite 'Help' wafting its way to us. At first we were sure that some freak breeze had carried towards us from the trail that was some 75 yards up above us. Then it started to get more insistent. Yep it was definitely a human voice and it was shouting in English. How did I know it was a shout? Have you ever heard of anyone in the mountains whispering for help?

It appeared to be coming from the trees on the rocky ledge. We trudged off to just bellow the ledge and lo and behold we found the rare sight of the Lesser

Spotted English Schoolboy half- way up one of the trees.

There he was, this poor sod frozen, he had been there for over an hour, hanging on for dear life. As 'tail end Charlie he had been happily following his ski class, they turned right, he didn't and went straight over the side, hurtled some 50 yards down through the deep snow shot through the air and ended up this tree. And I do mean up the tree. No half measures here in fact if he had been any higher he would have been mistaken for the Angel on a Christmas tree, apart from the spotty face that is.

Fortunately for him we came along otherwise he was in for a very long night. Getting him down was going to be a problem. The actual mechanics weren't the problem. No that was a simple matter of him letting go. The snow was deep enough to cushion his fall. No that wasn't the problem, getting the little bugger to let go of his tree was the challenge.

We pleaded, begged and argued to no avail. No way was he letting go of his tree. Finally, under the threat of us leaving, did he finally let go. Screaming like a Banshee he crashed through the lower branches and landed with a soft 'Plooff' in the snow some 20 feet bellow. The depth of the snow and steepness of the slope gave him a soft pillow of a landing. He re-emerged covered in snow. He looked as if he suffered from really bad dandruff. We dusted him off and managed to get down just in time to catch the last lift up and, thankfully, stop a dragnet of intrepid ski patrollers ready to set out looking for him.

I often wonder if his friends believed him when he told them he was up a tree.

At least this time I knew why this guy was in a strange place.

THE VAN

At the end of my last season in Scotland I bought an old VW van. It was one of the ubiquitous split windscreen dormobile vans circa 1960. It was green and cream- weren't they all that colour? Kind of Fordian, they can have any colour they like, so long as it's... that is until the Hippies got their sweaty little hands on them. They're probably one of the most enduring symbols synonymous with the Flower Power era. That must have really grated on Germanic sensibilities.

My girlfriend Catherine and I were going to spend some time travelling around Europe. (This is a way I would suggest to travel for any youngster, especially in-between college and getting a real job.) I had a summer job teaching watersports just outside of St. Tropez in the South of France. The winter would take care of itself; it was too far away to worry about.

We set off and it wasn't too long before we discovered that we had a wee problem. Unless our battery was super duper charged there was just enough dirt in the starter solenoid to stop it from engaging the starter motor all we got was an insipid "Clunk!" No big problem, only two bolts hold the starter motor in place on most engines and the VW was no exception. The unfortunate thing was, as I was soon to discover, we would have to move the whole engine to create space to get the bloody thing out. It stayed where it was.

We found a solution, Catherine would turn the ignition key while I rolled under the vehicle and belted the starter motor with a bloody great spanner. It worked a treat. This was to be our modus operandi for the rest of our epic trip. Needless to say we got some weird looks all over Europe. We had it down to a fine art even when the engine would die at traffic lights I could be out, under, Whack! And back in the driver's seat before the lights changed.

I actually got an ovation at an Italian Gas Station. We pulled in to fill up and I had a desperate need to go and wash my hands. Leaving Catherine to fill up I walked with that stiff-legged gait and six inch stride that afflicts all people in my situation. That feeling of wanting to rush, but terrified to make any kind of sudden movement or, Heaven forbid any kind of jarring movement.

When I reappeared, Catherine and the van were surrounded by madly gesticulating Italian men- well they do don't they. Apparently after she had filled up, well I was gone for a wee (pun intended) while, well my hands were very dirty, they had asked her to move the van forward. Stalwart that she was, she immediately jumped in, turned the ignition key and was met with the expected insipid 'Clank'. Giving her sweetest smile, it is a beaut', a shrug of the shoulders and she soon had men coming to her aid from every corner of the forecourt.

By the time I arrived I had to practically fight my way

through. Grabbing the usual spanner I rolled under...'Whack!' the engine roared into life and I emerged to thunderous applause. I think I may have even been offered job. After surviving a deluge of slaps on the back we set off again.

Don't think that this story of the trial and tribulations of travelling around in a van is unique. Nearly all the people we met had similar tales to tell. One couple nearly got arrested in Switzerland, for breaking into their own van. For some reason VW in its wisdom gave a different key for all the doors and the ignition. This pair had lost all the keys except for the ignition and the little door at the back. They were touring Europe entering and exiting via the little rear door. It was during the contortion phase, well it is a small door and they were quite tall, that the Police nearly arrested them. It took a lot of convincing on their part before they were allowed to go on their way. Oh it's an adventure all right, but fun.

Half way through the summer we noticed that we were getting close to needing new tyres. We were on the verge of buying a new set when we had a stroke of luck. We had to go up into the mountains to visit one of the nearby ski resorts. As chance would have it there was a total wreck of a van. It had rolled halfway down the mountain, but unlike a Hollywood vehicle it hadn't immediately burst into flames and blown up, no it was just lying on it's back like a dead Beetle. (intentional VW joke!) We returned South with brand spanking new tyres. The fact that the rear two tyres were of the studded winter variety didn't bother us one whit.

The summer season ended and we did some travelling around. It was great stopping where and when you liked. We stopped one evening in Turin. It was dark and once we parked I left Catherine and went to reconnoitre the immediate area. A habit I picked up from my time in the Army. To my astonishment when I returned to the van it was literally surrounded by 'Peeping Toms!' I actually had to elbow my way through. Only when I reappeared from the van brandishing a big Scuba Diver's knife did they reluctantly dispersed, really weird. Catherine was blissfully unaware of what was going on. What did they see...Catherine reading a book.

We wended our way through Italy and started to head up towards Switzerland. Passing through Ciavenna we threaded our way through the Mountains to the border control. The distance between the Italian and Swiss border posts is about 25 yards. We were waved past the Italian side by a smiling but thoroughly disinterested border guard. The Swiss Guard started giving us a good look. After circling us several times he appeared at my window.
"You have winter tyres."

"Yes." I said with pride.

"But this is October and you are not permitted to use studded tyres in Switzerland until November."

Oops. That ol' deflated feeling was descending fast.

"Ah, er, well we're only passing through." I tried.

His eyes rolled in his head. "Maybe but you've still got to use hundreds of kilometres of our roads."

Touché.

"Okay but where can I change my tyres here?" My riposte.

At that he smiled and pointed to a garage some fifty yards into Switzerland. I bet his Bother owned it. Anyway I know when I'm beaten, but it does not take a rocket scientist to realise that tyres in the land of William Tell and Cuckoo clocks was going to be expensive. So I smiled and said.

"No we'll get them back in Italy."

He shrugged and walked away leaving me to do a three-point turn and head back. A 1960 VW is a heavy brute and these types of manoeuvres are by no means simple. But we were soon heading back towards our previously uninterested border guard. Guess what...yeah he was no longer so disinterested, was he. Neither were about half a dozen of his mates as we headed towards Italy, some five minutes after we had left it.

"Why are the Swiss not letting you in?"

"Oh it's just because we've got studded tyres."
A glint came into his eyes.

"You can't come into Italy with studded tyres."

Aaaargh! I had visions of being trapped in 25-sq. yards of no-man's land. I think my mouth opened but no sound came out. We were left hung out dry for what seemed ages then they burst out laughing and waved us through. We must have made their day.

We eventually made it to Austria where I got a job in a Ski School. Catherine declined an offer of work from them and found herself a job as a secretary.

There are lots of things to try in Austria but the next two should have a Government health warning. Jäger Tea and Ströh Rum. Remember you were warned here. These are two lethal tipples, as I was to find out.
One night after a few of the premier I started on the latter. Wrong move, oh such a wrong move. According to legend somewhere between one and two in the morning I was bewailing the colour of our van. Green and cream was boring, I had enough of it, it was time for a change. So, drunk as a Skunk and armed with the remnants of a bottle of Rum, a tin of Black paint and a paintbrush-yes a paintbrush, I don't even want to know where I got them from. I attacked the van, and in the dark I happily

repainted our VW.

The following morning I awoke, which was deemed a feat in itself, not even a Shakespeare, Milton or Keats would have had the ability to describe my 'Hang over'. Possibly Owen with his WWI experiences might have come close, but me, I have no chance. I staggered out into the morning sunlight to be confronted by the new look van.

"AAAaaargh! Who the hell did that?"

"You did, you daft b***r."

I was eloquently informed. I couldn't deny it. I was covered in as much paint as the van. The snow around had not escaped either.

You have been warned.
Stay away from JT and SR.

A NIGHT ON THE PERNOD

This evening in particular seems to have stuck in the minds of quite a few people. It involves a guy called Bill, myself and an awful lot of Pernod.

Bill and I were enjoying a raucous evening. The company was great, as we would say in Scotland "The crack was great." We were in fine form and feeling no pain.

Pernod was the tipple of the Evening, a habit I had acquired working in La Belle France. Actually I started drinking it when I was informed that it was an aphrodisiac. It's a lie I had ten last night and only nine worked! I jest of course, but Dogs (The 4 legged variety) tend to follow you home. Something to do with the smell of aniseed I believe. Whatever we were getting tore into a bottle of the stuff.

As the night progressed we finished the bottle in our usual watering hole and were informed that they didn't have another bottle. With the indignation that only drunks can muster we left and repaired to the bar upstairs, some two flights of stairs away. We had reached the stage where we would order a drink to have while we waited for our drinks order to be filled at the bar. Can't go thirsty waiting for the Barman to pour your drinks can you. Oh we took our drinking seriously.
By 10 o'clock we had finished another bottle and were in a fine state. We knew how much we had to drink as the

next day the Bar Staff, with great relish told us. We were the only ones drinking Pernod so it was a pretty easy affair for them to keep 'score'.

Closing time came and we decided that we'd visit a hotel some five miles away as it was having a Disco and...a late bar.
How we got there is shrouded in mystery. I think I like it that way.

"Right Bill, I know a way through the kitchens. We can get in without paying."

"Sounds good to me."

Off we staggered to the back of the Hotel. It's true, when sober I did know (most of the locals knew of it) the way through. It was a pretty simple affair, all we had to do was hop over the hotplate- yes it would be switched off- and the door from the kitchen opened right onto the dance floor. I primed Bill with this information with an added proviso that if we encountered a cleaner or someone of that ilk, we just walk by as if we've got every right to be there. No problems and off we set. As it was there was a cleaner there who watched the whole episode unfold before him.

Now when I said I knew the way the key word was 'sober' which of course I wasn't and proceeded to get hopelessly lost. Only a drunk could get lost in a small kitchen...guilty as charged. Eventually we stumbled towards a door.

"This is it." I said with complete certainty.

"Now remember we barge straight in and onto the dance floor."

Bill just nodded. I think at this stage he had temporarily lost the power of speech. We braced, then one behind the other we burst through the door and almost at once skidded to a stop, there was a bloody great aeroplane coming straight for us. It was the Cinema! As we looked to our right we saw about a hundred pairs of eyes looking at us. We did a quick exit to the rear.

Some friends were in the audience and told us it this way. About half an hour into the film, Airport or something akin, hence I hadn't been hallucinating. The door suddenly flew open and these two figures lurched in, screeched to a halt, a la 'Tom and Jerry' gaped open mouthed around them and then preceded to walk, well more like tried to tiptoe backwards...backwards mark you, and out of the cinema with the audience in hysterics. Well I'm glad we added to the evening's cabaret but we still hadn't penetrated the Disco.

Round we went to the front. We were on a mission now. We took a timeout to try and play some table tennis - now that is something I would have liked to have seen myself because by then I don't think either of us could have bitten our finger nails - From all accounts we had the Hotel Patrons in stitches. I must say at this point, we were happy drunks. After this short respite of sporting activity we got back to planning our assault on the dance.

In drunken whispers, which meant anyone within 50 feet was a party to our plans. A crowd was gathering. Even the manager came to watch. Completely unaware of all this we continued.

The Disco was being held in one of the dinning rooms that was at a slightly lower level than the foyer we were in. A passageway of about three people wide and some thirty feet long led to a flight of five steps that led down to the lower level. The actual door stood some six feet from the bottom of these steps. Behind the door sat three ticket sellers, who were also watching us with interest.

This was a cunning- in a 'Baldrician' tradition-Plan. We were going to run as fast as we could and we'd be through the door and mingling on the dance floor before they could react. With plans like this we could have been Generals in the First World War.

Plan set!
Egged on by a partisan crowd.
We took off!

For the people at the door we must have been a horrendous sight bearing down on them. I'll let you use your own imagination on the effects five steps would have on speeding drunks. It speaks volumes for the agility of the doormen to get out of the way and- God Bless 'em- open the two Glass doors before we two idiots became mincemeat. We thundered passed them almost on our knees and noses a few inches from the ground.

It took us all of the bar space, dance floor and the wall at the other end to regain our balance. As it was we still hit the wall with a Splat. But we had done it, we were IN.

We're were in...we're...out!!

Pleased as Punch we were. Of course we had completely ignored the fact that it was our Ski School's Disco and we were getting in for free anyway.

Duh!

Anybody know any Blonde jokes?

T-BAR BLUES

Remember earlier in the book, I said, it was paramount that the instructor should try not to say something to his pupils that could be open to misinterpretation. Well here I get caught out beautifully.

For those of you that are too young or just new to the sport let me take some moments to explain what a T-Bar is. Fortunately it is a dying breed of ski lifts, not before time I may add. Basically you would stand, skis on, and be pulled up the slope. A rope hung down from a pulley attached to cable, at the bottom, the skier's end was a wooden stock in the shape of, would you believe, a T. It looked for all the world like an Anchor.

The lift operator would place the centre spar in-between two skiers and the cross spar under their bums. For instructors this was a nightmare. Pupils using the lift for the first time would see this as an invitation to sit down. It didn't matter often you told people not to sit, they would. Practically every time a beginners group was venturing up for the first time you'd see a poor instructor having apoplexy.
Shouts of

"Don't sit down! Stand up! I said don't sit down!...Oh sod it."
would ring out a warning that beginners were on the lift. Anyone with sense would then avoid that lift like the

plague.

As I said the theory was that the cross spar sat comfortably at your bottom. Good plan, however the chances of getting someone with a bum at the same height as your own, ah now there's a challenge. The bar was more likely to be around your ankles or in the nape of your neck. Oh they were great fun.

Being an adult brought an added pleasure, you were invariably asked to take a child up with you. Oh what joy, all the way up holding on to a kid with the bar at your ankles. If you managed to survive the initial Jerk you'd be sweating cobblers by the time you got the top and one arm would have been all but rendered useless.

At the arrival area the bar became absolutely lethal. There was a giant wheel lying horizontal overhead and the cable wound round this taking the bar from your grasp and swinging it around like a giant slingshot before taking it back down to the bottom for it's next victim. Woe betides anyone who lingered at the arrival area.

One pupil I had to take up (several times) had this amazing habit of leaning way out to the side and for several rides I had physically hold her on to the Damn thing. No amount of cajoling or pleading on my part could get her to stay in the middle. She just kept leaning away from the central spar. All my mates were having a great laugh watching me struggle up the hill-we're not talking about a petite young lady here. Making it worse, she wouldn't even hold on to the central spar.

After numerous trips up the lift, I realised that as long as I held her she would never make any attempt to stay on for herself plus I got fed up so let go.
Whoosh, off she shot.

She swears to this day, that I threw her off!! Fortunately the Boss of the Ski School was on the bar behind and saw the whole thing, whew.

These bars also had some surprises for the single traveller. On the longer lifts concentration would flag. People would get a bit Blasé and the bar, like the shark in Jaws, would strike.

The tracks of all draglifts become rutted and icy and sooner or later the unwary would hit ice or catch an edge. That's when the bar would become like something out of a Steven King movie. Unbeknown to our traveller the hook, what the T part of the Bar had now become, has found its way under the jacket and as they fall it hooks them like a Fly fisherman does a Trout. In their case more like a Flounder. With head down, bum up and jacket well and truly caught they carry on their relentless journey to the top. Every effort to shout is met with a mouth full of snow. Wonderful things T-Bars, invented by the Spanish Inquisition I think.

I had a great group; they were good fun and were

starting to ski the bumps. The dynamics of the group was optimum (in other words the 'crack' was great.) We had been skiing the bumps on the main run and stopped at the middle station for lunch. Opposite the restaurant was the T-Bar that serviced the run and I turned to the group and said. "I've got a private lesson now. I'll meet you at the T-Bar in an hour and a quarter."

"Aye, no problem Les we'll see you later." And they trudged off for lunch.

I finished the private lesson and got to the meeting area about 5 minutes early. The appointed time comes and goes...no group. 10 minutes...No group...20 minutes and finally half an hour passes, still no group so off I go in search of them. Ski School office, nope, First Aid room, happily no. Finally I head towards the Café. There they all were.

"Hi Les we were getting worried. Where have you been?"

"Where have I been...Wh...I said we'd meet at the T-Bar."

"But Les,
we are at the Tea Bar!"

T.V. COMES TO TOWN

There was a time when we used to get TV programmes coming up to Aviemore to film some of their ski sequences-before they discovered they could get better expenses Abroad. One memorable occasion they chose a rather large New Zealander. He had a barrel chest, which fitted quite well with his barrel of beer belly. He also had the skinniest legs I've ever seen on anyone of his stature. We were constantly amazed that they held him up, they looked like a couple of threads with knots in them. But at just under six feet he was an imposing figure.

He was to be dressed up as a pirate, he was a 'Goody' and was going to be filmed being chased by a few other instructors dressed as the 'Baddies'. For the climax he was to whoosh down a gentle slope, come to a stop at the back of a huge billboard and push his head through the specially prepared thin paper. He would then be substituted for the real actor.

Everything was prepared, a gap at the bottom had been prepared to allow his skis to pass underneath and stop at his bindings. Pretty simple stuff, but this was not taking into account a Kiwi all pumped up about being on the Telly, was it? Especially as he was going to be left hanging around for ages while the TV people 'fuffed' around. If you've never had anything to do with the making of movies or the like, keep it that way. It takes them forever to get their **** together.

Finally they were ready and someone shouted Action!- Honest they do. Down he came, as we all watched it became clear that he was coming down the slope a tad too fast. Crash! Scratch one billboard.

"Okay sweetie." Minced someone in charge.
"Can we try that again with just a little less oomph."

Another wait ensued but at least this time we could see why. There were splinters of wood all over the snow.

"Take 2 Action!"...Zoom... Crash!

"Take 3 Action!"...Whoosh...Crash!

The Set people were sweating and cursing as the repaired the Billboard after each 'Take'. The Board itself was beginning to look more like kindling for a fire. I lost count at 20.'Takes'. We were in hysterics. I didn't think I could laugh any more, it hurt. It was a very wobbly billboard by now. It says wonders for the skill of the set people that they kept managing to repair it. It was of course a shadow of it's former self. So was the 'Sweetie' I wished I had share in the company that made Valium. Seeing him unravel was almost as funny as watching our hero demolish the billboard.

Two men were now designated to hold the board, as there were no supports left on it. They were not the happiest of people...I don't blame them. Eventually to the relief of all involved they finally got the shot they wanted and we could repair to the bar and discuss the career prospects of the latest Douglas Fairbanks Jr.

My turn was to come but I was to dress up as a Womble.

Wombles were a very successful kids programme on British TV. It was about a family of these furry creatures living on Wimbledon common. They apparently picked up all the rubbish that humans unthinkingly littered the common with. Not a bad message for kids. I know all this now but at the time I hadn't a clue. But there I was dressed in this furry suit.

There were three of us designated for the job, yours truly, a Frenchman called Bernard and another Scot called Dave.

Bernard was over for the season to improve his English. He was a delightful character. He kept a little notebook where he compiled a list of useful phrases in English. He had all the pages designated into specific categories. Pages one and two related to skiing, thee and four to climbing and so on.

Page six was the page for all the 'swear words' and rude phrases. Anyone that is learning, or has learned a new language will appreciate the fact that when you get excited or agitated it is very difficult to find these words in the new language. Bernard came up with a unique way around this, when he got agitated or angry he used to shout, "Page six!" Brilliant.

This caught on and were all going around giving it the "Why don't you page six off!" treatment. It was a hoot swearing at all and sundry...with impunity.

Dave made up the trio. He was a good Guy but boy did his feet smell. When he came into the changing room to get out of his ski boots there was a stampede for the door. I kid you not. Now I've been in the Army and I know a thing or six about smelly feet but this guy Wow - I'm sure he had to get surgically removed from his socks at the end of the season. Between the three of us we knew nothing of the Wombles, but there we were all togged out in furry suits, we were Wombles.

Anyone that thinks filming is exciting and glamorous has no idea how boring it can be. Hours of tedium followed by five minutes of action. It was like being back in the Army, hurry up and wait.

Now I'm a bit of a short arse so the crotch of my Womble suit was dragging in the snow. This created a wee bit of a problem when we had to ski over the camera. About six feet away from the camera I had to reach down grab the suit and pull it up high enough to pass over it, oh what fun. Having to go over this for numerous takes was not enhancing my thoughts of the movie industry.

During yet another lull in the proceedings I felt a tug at my leg. I looked down to be confronted by a kid of about six years old.

"Can I have your autograph?"

Who me... well of course not it was the Womble's signature he wanted, wasn't it. No problem, except there was...er...which Womble was I?

I looked at Dave, he shrugged, not a clue. I looked towards Bernard...Why, if we didn't know he would have 'page six' all chance of knowing would he? Uncle Bulgaria was the only name I knew so that's the name I signed.

The Kid took the paper, looked at the scrawl and said.

"You're not Uncle Bulgaria. You're Wellington!" With that he let fly a kick at my leg and ran off. Bloody Hell one day in the Movies and already I had critics.

Eventually they found a piece of terrain that they wanted us to ski down. They couldn't have found a trickier spot to ski if they'd have searched all season. It was a narrow strip with rocks showing through on either side. I will say that it wasn't all their fault as Mother Nature (Is that a sexist name?) was being her unpredictable fickle self (Okay now I'm sure it is) and had not given us too much snow to choose from. Finally the cameras were all set up and we were in position.

"Action!"

Off we thundered. I went about two turns when I discovered a glitch. It was quite a big glitch in fact. The head of a Womble has a long snout and our eyeholes were some way down said snout.

The problem? As soon as we picked up speed wind got under the schnozzle lifting it up and thus giving me a lovely view of… nothing! I could see 'Page 6' all.

How we made down to the bottom without being impaled on a rock I'll never know. I ended up with one hand holding the end of the nose down to give me some kind of visibility. We stood around at the bottom muttering when a voice chirped in.

"Wonderful 'Dahlings'. Can we do another take?"

We were about to tell him, collectively to 'Page six' off, then we thought of hanging around for another couple of hours. We went back up. Seven times we went back up. For the life of me I could tell no difference between any of them. No wonder film budgets go over.

The show was scheduled for a Christmas Special. We invited all our mates around for a party and to watch our derring-do's on the Small Screen. Well any excuse for a party. On came the show, here comes the Wombles segment, any minute now, blink, did you miss it?

All day 'Dicking' around for less than 10 seconds! We were gob smacked. A sarcastic voice piped up.

"About sums up your sex life, don't it."

He had put it all beautifully into perspective and we started to hoot with laughter and...Party.

LES, THE DJ (?)

It was the start of a new season and I was made one of the resident instructors at the Badenoch Hotel. The other ski teacher, Peter was from New Zealand. He was the opposite from me. He had a steady girlfriend (he later married her) and had been a ski teacher for over ten years and the novelty of the job had kinda worn off for him. Me, I was still like a dog let loose in a forest.

This was a pretty good deal as it meant we got our evening meals for free in the dinning hall with the guests. All we had to do was be on call in the bar to answer any of the hotel guest's questions. It was an arduous task sitting in the bar for a couple of hours. Still someone had to do it. Unfortunately the chef was going through a 'Nouvelle Cuisine' phase.

Our first night we sat down at the table drooling in anticipation. Our jaws dropped when our plates were placed before us. We were looking at something that belonged in the Tate gallery – in the miniatures section! I mean it was pretty to look at but it was also pretty damn small! We had been out skiing for six hours. We needed food not this piece of modern art that was placed before us. Just like modern art – it didn't make any sense.

Fortunately, I knew some of the folks that worked in the kitchen so I nipped in to see them.

'Hi Les!' one of the sous-chefs greeted me.

'Something wrong with the food?' He asked.

"Nah, the food's great there's just not enough of it. You know we've been out in sub- zero temperatures all day."

"Say no more." And with that he started to heap my plate up and off I trundled back to my table.

It was a hoot to watch the envious faces of the other diners as Pete and I tucked into plates heaped with food while they sat with their Nouvelle cuisine.

Things were going fine. We were giving the staff free ski lessons and the use of our ski rental gear and in return we had carte blanche to go into the kitchen and help ourselves. This also applied in the restaurant 'The Buttery' which was open to the public. There we'd order from the kiddies menu and get huge servings at the cheaper price. A great arrangement.

I also discovered what happens to diners who were pains in the ass. Now if someone has a genuine complaint and comments in the correct way, in general, they get treated with sympathy. However there is always the one who is just obnoxious. Whether they are doing it to impress someone or are just normally like that it matters not a jot. The fact that they are rude is enough.

The first time it happened I was standing in the kitchen helping myself to more spuds when the door slammed open, in stormed a waiter. He waited 'til he was sure he was out of earshot of the dining room and then let rip.

"That a**hole is at again! The steak's not done well enough, the jerk asked for a rare steak and now he says it's too bloody" at that the steak went on an 'Orvil Wright.' It flew through the air with the greatest of ease and plopped at the feet of a sous-chef. He promptly stood on it then picked it up and put it on the grill.

"Vengeance is mine." Sayeth the sous-chef

At that point I made a mental note to always be polite to waiters.

We were a couple of weeks into the season and we had a meeting with the manager of the hotel. He wanted to do something to attract people to the Viking Bar. This was the hotel bar that was open to the public. He wanted something that would attract people for just after skiing. A good Après Ski evening. I don't remember who came up with the idea of a drinking competition but that's what was decided on.

It wasn't to be a straight forward 'Who can drink a pint of beer the quickest.' Oh no, it was decided that it would be a hoot if they had to quaff a bottle of beer through the teat of a baby's bottle. Thus it was christened 'The Baby Boozer.'

"Right Les we want you to be the emcee." He gushed.

" We won't pay you but all your drinks are free."

At this the barman nearly had apoplexy.
Me I thought I'd died and gone to heaven. Free food and free booze! Hold me back!

Then came his next surprise, he had bought a DJ's turntable so I could play music as well. No problem except that he only had about 15 single tracks and about 10 LP's. We're talking vinyl here folks.

Still the Baby Boozer was only supposed to last for about an hour to an hour and a half and for most of that I'd be yakking on the microphone so that should be enough.

Of course at the mention of a beer drinking competition we got all the bruisers coming in with tales of downing a pint in three seconds etcetera. Well the look on their faces when they realized they had to suck it through the baby tit. Out bloody standing, that look of disbelief was worth the admission on it's own.

At this juncture I'd like say that one of the fastest persons that I have ever watched down a beer was a girl called Thea. She was one of the instructors and I once had the misfortune of being against her in a boat race.

Now for the few of you that don't know what a boat race is here's an explanation.

There are two or more teams. (Any number of players) You stand in a line facing your opposite number. It starts at one end when both leaders down their pint. When they've finished they hold their glass upside down over their head. As soon as the leader has put their glass over their head the number two of the team can start drinking their pint and thus they work their way through their team. Like a relay race. The next drinker can't start until the person before him turns his glass upside over their head. If you don't mind getting wet you can cheat..

Now I'm hopeless at drinking beer fast but I was once cajoled into joining a team. I looked across and there was Thea who was to be my drinking opponent. Now I figured that she couldn't be any faster than me. Boy was I wrong. I didn't even get the glass to my lips. She just poured it straight down. Quite a few jaws dropped I can tell you. Me I cheated and got awfully wet! And Thea? Well she got the biggest cheer of the night.

'The Baby Boozer' became quite successful and started to attract ski teachers from other ski schools and locals to come and watch the festivities. I even got the DeeJaying thing down. Well it wouldn't have been recognizable to any aficionado but it worked for us.

Basically we had about eight good dance tunes I would

play them and everybody would dance. Once I had gone through these I'd put on an LP then we'd **all** (Yup me too) repair to the Bar. The LP would finish I'd go back up, play the good tunes again then back to the bar. This went on 'til closing. It was a hoot. (And Barbara if you read this I can still see your blonde hair cascading around as you danced.)

My last stint was a classic. It was almost the end of the season and we had a challenge soccer match between the instructors and the trainers. We had a hoot kicking lumps out of each other and drinking cans of beer together on the sideline. A great day was had by all.

Unfortunately as is usual at the end of the seasons there are lots of parties going on and inevitably they over-lap. Today was to be a duzy.

Right after the soccer match the Ski School owner was having an end of season cocktail party at his house. No time to change so we turned up in soccer gear. Sandy's a great guy and he didn't give a hoot how we arrived. He was just glad to see us. He had even got in a bottle of Pernod especially for me. This was now officially mine and I set off to find a glass big enough. I found this humongous brandy glass. I was in hog heaven.

It was a great party unfortunately it was also the night of the last 'Baby Boozer' of the season so still in soccer gear and of course now armed with my huge brandy glass of Pernod off we went to the Viking Bar.

It was a riotous affair. However at one stage someone came up to complain that I had been playing the same song several times. There I was sitting in my soccer gear, soccer boots, dirty knees trying to look serious (and focus) as I listened to this oink.

Apparently I'd been putting a new disc on the turntable but by the time the music stopped I couldn't remember (or see!!) which one had been played so I had been taking the new one off and replaying the one that had just been on. Go figure.

It shows how much fun we were having as **he** was the only one that had noticed!

Feeling No Pain!

Thus sitting in my soccer gear,
cradling a huge brandy glass full of Pernod,

I ended my career as a DJ.

DREAM JOB
&
THE 'JOURNALIST' (?)

It was my third year at the French Ski School when Yves the Boss came to me one day in January.

"Les there are some English journalists outside will you show them around for the day."

No problem, out I went to meet them.
This skinny, weedy character introduced himself (for the life of me I can't remember his name) I'm from the Sun he informed me.

"Sorry I thought I was meeting a journalist."

Well I thought I get the day off to a good start. You know how occasionally you meet someone and there is an instant rapport, well this wasn't one of them. I can not explain it but I took an instant dislike to this guy. Completely irrational, he had done nothing or said anything to upset me but there it was, dislike. The other lad was a different kettle of fish. He was the photographer and he was a good bloke.

They were here to do a story on what goes on in a typical Ski Resort. Would I let them do an interview?

Not a chance, however I would introduce them around and if anyone did want to be quoted (Or misquoted as was more likely the case) well that was up to them. I took them around the Bars and quite a few people were delighted to tell a few stories. In one Bar they positioned everyone for a group photograph, took their names, bought a few beers and sat back and listened.

Weeks later I was to see a copy of the article that appeared in the paper. They literally destroyed the reputation of one of the girls. They accredited me with a story that I had never heard before. So guess my initial 'Gut feeling' was right after all. I felt really sorry for the girl. She was actually a 'nice' girl but the story made her out to be some kind of slag, screwing around with a different guy each night. Complete Crap. This weed of a character had created all kinds of heartache for a girl and her family. It was a cowardly attack on someone that he knew couldn't fight back.

There should be a way for people to defend themselves against sleaze balls like that (How about letting them punch the "journalists" on the nose. Having their faces rearranged a few times would make them think twice. I'd vote for that.) I mean who reads retractions done in small print and hidden among the ads for trusses and incontinence knickers? If you're going to write fiction, use fictitious people.
I at least got a form of compensation. They wanted someplace that they could take photographs of their 'page three Girl.' Now this has nothing in common with

Bernard's page six routine no the Sun created a British institution "The Page Three Girl." Everyday since the seventies there has been a photograph of a 'Topless' girl adorning page three of their tabloid paper. Some of these girls have become quite famous and wealthy- which says volumes for our society.

Imagine becoming rich by getting your Boobs photographed. It is quite mind boggling, but today I wasn't going to complain.

What they needed was somewhere off the beaten track where they could be left in peace to do a photo shoot. I knew the exact spot.

First we went to collect the Lady and she was stunning. If anything she actually looked better in the flesh (sic) than in the subsequent photos. We walked a little way into the woods and found the ideal spot. There was a flat area followed by a gentle slope of some 15 feet and then another flat section. Perfect. However there was a little problem...she had never put skis on in her life.

I'm not being gallant when I say that I thought that it was brave of her, dressed or undressed, as she was to even contemplate sliding down on skis. But she was up for it.
There was no other solution, I would have to walk her up to the start, slide back down to the bottom and there, horror of horrors wait for her to slide down. I would then have the arduous task of catching her.

in this instance I didn't mind having to do numerous 'Takes'.

TRUST ME.

I'LL CATCH YOU!

And to think my Mum used to ask me
why I didn't get a real job!!!

Hi

I hope you've enjoyed this first collection 'Tales.' from my ski years.

Look out for the Tales from my summer jobs.

From working in the south of France to the Alps and beyond!

That...Oh sh**t! Moment

OUT SOON.

Cheers
Les

Also from Les is;

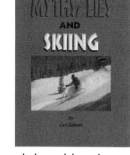

'MYTHS, LIES and SKIING' is an acclaimed book on the easiness inherent in learning to ski .

The Chairman of the Austrian Ski Instructors Association who called it *"A priceless jewel."* and had it translated into Germen to distribute it to his ski instructors. Many Austrian ski schools followed suit.

It will revolutionize the way people perceive skiing and ski instruction. Skiing really is easy to do. Too many people struggle round the slopes. Les passionately wants to change that.

"The most inspirational ski book" and *"At last a book people can learn from. All ski instructors should read it."*

These are just some of the comments from skiers and instructors.

Printed in Great Britain
by Amazon.co.uk, Ltd.,
Marston Gate.